SPORTS

SPORTS

Biblical
TRUTHS
— for —
Competitors

B&H
PUBLISHING GROUP
NASHVILLE, TENNESSEE

Copyright © 2018 by B&H Publishing Group
All Rights Reserved
Printed in the United States of America

978-1-5359-1776-6

Published by B&H Publishing Group
Nashville, Tennessee

Dewey Decimal Classification: 242.5
Subject Heading: DEVOTIONAL LITERATURE \
BIBLE—INSPIRATION \ MEDITATIONS \ PRAYERS

1 2 3 4 5 6 7 8 • 22 21 20 19 18

CONTENTS

CONTENTS

Sports are one of the greatest connectors in our world today. It's one of the things that we can all be a part of. No matter what team you belong to, there is always a shared comradery for the appreciation of the sport you follow. It's one of the places people can learn the deepest of life-lessons. Whether you're an athlete, a coach, or just a fan, you've probably come to know that sports have more weight than just competition. They also can hold a great deal of the biblical truths we try to apply in our daily lives.

Many athletes will tell you of great moments during their athletic careers. They may mention a touchdown, a winning shot, or a play that made the difference between a win and a loss. There will be other moments, however, that hold just as high a significance: a loss, a moment of failure, a missed shot, or a bad call. Others may not mention either. They may mention the wise words from a coach, a squabble that had been left on the field, or a lesson learned while training. Whatever the occasion, athletes always seem to hold onto those moments within their own personal highlight reel. Allow the Scriptures to show the deeper meaning hiding behind the sports we've come to know and love.

ANGER

There is nothing worse than losing a game you knew you were going to win. Ask an athlete, coach, or fan. They will most likely be able to point to a moment where they experienced rage most have never seen. We've all seen coaches scream, athletes throw equipment, or fans hit furniture. There's a reason they call it an upset, after all. Most of us agree that we shouldn't act like that, but somehow it happens. Anger is something that is going to pop up from time to time. It's a reaction, but it is not something we should let stay, or worse, allow it to grow.

Refrain from anger and give up your rage;
do not be agitated—it can only bring harm.
    Psalm 37:8

———

A patient person shows great understanding,
but a quick-tempered one promotes foolishness.
    Proverbs 14:29

———

A gentle answer turns away anger,
but a harsh word stirs up wrath.
    Proverbs 15:1

"But I tell you, everyone who is angry with his brother or sister will be subject to judgment. Whoever insults his brother or sister, will be subject to the court. Whoever says, 'You fool!' will be subject to hellfire."

Matthew 5:22

———

Be angry and do not sin. Don't let the sun go down on your anger, and don't give the devil an opportunity.

Ephesians 4:26–27

Lord, I am angry. I expected something to happen one way and it happened another. I am frustrated over what is happening in my life right now. Father, ease my angry heart and fill it with a spirit of peace and understanding. Take this anger from me, Father, and guide me to a place of joy with You. Amen

Being a referee is one of the most difficult jobs in the game. You probably see a referee get screamed at by a player or a coach at least once every game you've seen. Whenever we hear the whistle blown out of turn, we're not normally happy when we see those black and white stripes running toward us, but there is still an understood respect for the referee because of his authority on the field. It is this lesson that teaches us that there are those in our lives that do have authority over us. They normally have knowledge, experience, or wisdom that you don't. Respect the authority of those that God has placed over you; they will normally have a wisdom to share that you haven't thought about.

Then he said to them, "Give, then, to Caesar the things that are Caesar's, and to God the things that are God's." When they heard this, they were amazed. So they left him and went away.

Matthew 22:21–22

———

Jesus came near and said to them, "All authority has been given to me in heaven and on earth."

Matthew 28:18

———

Let everyone submit to the governing authorities, since there is no authority except from God, and the authorities that exist are instituted by God.

Romans 13:1

*For this reason God highly exalted him and gave
him the name that is above every name, so that at
the name of Jesus every knee will bow—in heaven
and on earth and under the earth—and every
tongue will confess that Jesus Christ is Lord, to the
glory of God the Father.*

    Philippians 2:9–11

———

*Submit to every human authority because of
the Lord, whether to the emperor as the supreme
authority or to governors as those sent out by him
to punish those who do what is evil and to praise
those who do what is good. For it is God's will that
you silence the ignorance of foolish people by doing
good.*

    1 Peter 2:13–15

Father, teach me to respect the authority of those You have put over me. Allow me to view these people with a learning heart and a willingness to grow from their teachings. Lord, allow me to recognize and submit to Your authority in my life. Allow me to submit to that authority and have it be the leadership in my life. Amen

There is something about the bond between athlete and coach. One of the worst things that can happen on the field is a life-changing injury. Most athletes have seen at least one, but there's always something hidden within the tragedy that changes the nature of the game forever: compassion. Every now and again, you hear about a coach that spent the night at a hospital just to know that his player is ok, or you'll hear about teammates that mow the yard for the parents of the injured player, or how the community will jump into the lives of the people to support them with whatever they need. Allow the Bible to reinforce that compassion that comes from your team.

Yet he was compassionate;
he atoned for their iniquity
and did not destroy them.
He often turned his anger aside
and did not unleash all his wrath.
  Psalm 78:38

———

When he went ashore, he saw a large crowd and
had compassion on them, because they were like
sheep without a shepherd. Then he began to teach
them many things.
  Mark 6:34

Carry one another's burdens; in this way you will fulfill the law of Christ.

Galatians 6:2

———

And be kind and compassionate to one another, forgiving one another, just as God also forgave you in Christ.

Ephesians 4:32

Heavenly Father, my heart is hard. Soften it. Allow me to move with compassion for other people. Give me the moments that allow me to show the love that is needed. Father, thank You for the compassion and understanding that has been shown to me, and allow me to give the same to those around me that need it. Amen

Every once in a while, a team will play a game that they know they are going to win. Is this cockiness? Sometimes, but more often than not, it's because of preparation. A good team will go over the plays and strategies of their opponents and practice their own plays against them over and over until they know that victory is going to be the result of their practice. Are confidence and cockiness similar? Yes, but confidence is the knowledge of success because of the preparation and knowledge behind it. Cockiness is just the blind expectation of triumph. The same goes for our Christian walk; our time in prayer, the Word, and in worship are all indicators of one's preparation for a successful relationship with God.

Do not fear, for I am with you; do not be afraid, for I am your God. I will strengthen you; I will help you; I will hold on to you with my righteous right hand.

    Isaiah 41:10

———

It is not that we are competent in ourselves to claim anything as coming from ourselves, but our adequacy is from God.

    2 Corinthians 3:5

———

I am able to do all things through him who strengthens me.

    Philippians 4:13

So don't throw away your confidence, which has a great reward. For you need endurance, so that after you have done God's will, you may receive what was promised.

Hebrews 10:35–36

———

This is how we will know that we belong to the truth and will reassure our hearts before him whenever our hearts condemn us; for God is greater than our hearts, and he knows all things. Dear friends, if our hearts don't condemn us, we have confidence before God and receive whatever we ask from him because we keep his commands and do what is pleasing in his sight.

1 John 3:19–22

Lord God, thank You for all that You continue to do in my life. Thank You for giving me the opportunities in my life that have given me confidence. Father, I pray that You continue to work through me so that I may bless those around me. Lord, pour in me a spirit that drives me to pray more, to study Your Word, and to worship You more so that I may continue to walk in confidence with You. Amen

There is a natural conflict to sports. It's the very essence of competition, but an athlete will tell you that there's nothing worse than a conflict within the team. Most of us have seen this before. The quarterback has a bad relationship with his line, so he gets tackled more. The goalie was offended by something another player had said so he doesn't block as well. Whatever the reason, when there's conflict, the team doesn't perform as well as it should. Whenever there's conflict there is going to be a natural struggle in our ability to do what we need to do. This includes our relationship with Christ.

Therefore, putting away lying, speak the truth, each one to his neighbor, because we are members of one another. Be angry and do not sin. Don't let the sun go down on your anger, and don't give the devil an opportunity.

    Ephesians 4:25–27

———

"If your brother sins against you, go and rebuke him in private. If he listens to you, you have won your brother. But if he won't listen, take one or two others with you, so that by the testimony of two or three witnesses every fact may be established. If he doesn't pay attention to them, tell the church. If he doesn't pay attention even to the church, let him be like a Gentile and a tax collector to you."

    Matthew 18:15–17

A gentle answer turns away anger,
but a harsh word stirs up wrath.

    Proverbs 15:1

———

Bless those who persecute you; bless and do not
curse. Rejoice with those who rejoice; weep with
those who weep. Live in harmony with one another.
Do not be proud; instead, associate with the
humble. Do not be wise in your own estimation.
Do not repay anyone evil for evil. Give careful
thought to do what is honorable in everyone's eyes.
If possible, as far as it depends on you, live at peace
with everyone.

    Romans 12:14–18

Lord Jesus, please be with me. I am standing against someone I should love. My heart is hardening against others. Lord, instill in me a spirit of peace so that I may ease this conflict. Father, be with those that I have hurt. Allow them to find forgiveness for the wrong that I have done, and Father, allow me to find forgiveness for the wrong that has been done to me. Lord, put this conflict to rest and allow me to move forward with You. Amen

Most athletes will be able to tell you about a moment that they knew they were going to lose before they even started the game or match. Maybe the opposing team was bigger or faster; they had a star player that was clearly going to be a pro in the future, or they had a coach that had an intimidatingly impressive career. Whatever the reason, most athletes and coaches will tell you about that brief moment of fear, but what they all have in common is the same sentiment of "But we still played them with everything we had. . . ." Courage is more than just winning or losing; it's about standing up to the daunting, regardless of triumph or loss.

"Haven't I commanded you: be strong and courageous? Do not be afraid or discouraged, for the LORD your God is with you wherever you go."
  Joshua 1:9

———

I always let the LORD guide me.
Because he is at my right hand,
I will not be shaken.
  Psalm 16:8

———

Wait for the LORD;
be strong, and let your heart be courageous.
Wait for the LORD.
  Psalm 27:14

Be alert, stand firm in the faith, be courageous, be strong.

    1 Corinthians 16:13

———

For God has not given us a spirit of fear, but one of power, love, and sound judgment.

    2 Timothy 1:7

Father God, I am fearful of my future. I am worried that I may not be able to take on the things that may come my way. Father, please be with me. Give me the courage to take on the obstacles that are in my path. Instill in me a courageous spirit, Lord, so that I may be able to take on that which may come. Thank You, God, for giving me the courage to move forward in the times I am afraid to move at all. Amen

Most people know who the star athlete is. They're normally the one that's always in the game. Something that athlete has to deal with that most don't have to is the constant quality of courtesy. The true test of courtesy comes from how they handle conflicting situations. The moments where they are pulled out of a game so that less experienced players can have playing time will tell you a lot about the star player. If they are just talented, they will demand that they have all the time they can, but if they are a leader, they will exercise courtesy and allow others to improve.

Love one another deeply as brothers and sisters.
Outdo one another in showing honor.

    Romans 12:10

———

For the whole law is fulfilled in one statement: Love
your neighbor as yourself.

    Galatians 5:14

———

No foul language should come from your mouth, but
only what is good for building up someone in need,
so that it gives grace to those who hear.

    Ephesians 4:29

Let your speech always be gracious, seasoned with salt, so that you may know how you should answer each person.

    Colossians 4:6

———

Remind them to submit to rulers and authorities, to obey, to be ready for every good work, to slander no one, to avoid fighting, and to be kind, always showing gentleness to all people.

    Titus 3:1–2

Lord, teach me to be courteous. Give opportunities in my life so that I may be able to lead others. Allow me to lay down my pride, Lord, so that I may be courteous to others. Father, give me the discernment to recognize the opportunities to exercise courtesy. Instill in me a humble spirit to allow those around me the opportunity to grow. Amen

Deception happens in a game. There's nothing wrong with a good trick play, but that's as far as deception should go. One of the most important attributes for an athlete to have is honesty. If you cannot be trusted in your personal life, you will notice that your leadership will probably not be trusted on the team. If you cannot be trusted on the team, you will notice that your character will be questioned in your personal life. Deception has the ability to affect your life as a whole, even if you only exercise it in certain places.

The one who lives with integrity lives securely,
but whoever perverts his ways will be found out.
    Proverbs 10:9

———

"You are of your father the devil, and you want to
carry out your father's desires. He was a murderer
from the beginning and does not stand in the truth,
because there is no truth in him. When he tells a
lie, he speaks from his own nature, because he is a
liar and the father of lies."
    John 8:44

*Lying lips are detestable to the L*ORD*,*
but faithful people are his delight.
    Proverbs 12:22

Dear friends, do not believe every spirit, but test the
spirits to see if they are from God, because many
false prophets have gone out into the world.
    1 John 4:1

Lord Jesus, forgive me. I have deceived those around me. I have pretended to be something I am not. Lord, I know that I cannot live this way. I cannot expect to grow in you if I keep holding myself back with lies. Father, allow me to come clean to those that I've deceived. Please allow them to forgive me for the wrong I've done. Instill in me a spirit of honesty, Lord. Have me walk in truth and put deception to rest. Amen

The ability to encourage is one of the most
important things that a player or coach
can have. Sometimes all a player needs is
the reassurance that they can overcome the
obstacles of the game. Sometimes it comes
from a coach, but sometimes an encouraging
word can hold the same weight or more
coming from a teammate. It doesn't take a lot
to encourage, but it can mean the world to the
one being encouraged.

The Lord is the one who will go before you. He will be with you; he will not leave you or abandon you. Do not be afraid or discouraged.

Deuteronomy 31:8

———

God is our refuge and strength,
a helper who is always found
in times of trouble.

Psalm 46:1

———

"Aren't five sparrows sold for two pennies? Yet not one of them is forgotten in God's sight. Indeed, the hairs of your head are all counted. Don't be afraid; you are worth more than many sparrows."

Luke 12:6–7

"I have told you these things so that in me you may have peace. You will have suffering in this world. Be courageous! I have conquered the world."

    John 16:33

———

And let us watch out for one another to provoke love and good works, not neglecting to gather together, as some are in the habit of doing, but encouraging each other, and all the more as you see the day approaching.

    Hebrews 10:24–25

Father, thank You for putting those in my life that encourage me. Thank you for the words that people share that drive me to be better. Lord, allow me to take the encouraging moments that have been given to me, and allow me to share that same spirit of encouragement with others. Father, give me the ability to bring others up and not pull them down. Allow me to build people up and not break them down. Amen

Faith revolves around the notion that no matter what we do, where we are, or what we are going through, God is faithful. This doesn't mean that your team is going to win every game if your faith is strong enough. It simply means that God is enough. Instead of putting your faith in your team, put your trust in Him, and it will never be betrayed.

*Because of the L*ORD*'s faithful love*
we do not perish,
for his mercies never end.
They are new every morning;
great is your faithfulness!
     Lamentations 3:22–23

———

"Whoever is faithful in very little is also faithful in much, and whoever is unrighteous in very little is also unrighteous in much. So if you have not been faithful with worldly wealth, who will trust you with what is genuine? And if you have not been faithful with what belongs to someone else, who will give you what is your own?"
     Luke 16:10–12

"His master said to him, 'Well done, good and faithful servant! You were faithful over a few things; I will put you in charge of many things. Share your master's joy.'"
  Matthew 25:21

———

If we are faithless, he remains faithful, for he cannot deny himself.
  2 Timothy 2:13

———

Let us hold on to the confession of our hope without wavering, since he who promised is faithful.
  Hebrews 10:23

Father, give me faith. Give me faith to know that whatever may come, You always will be. Lord, instill in me a desire to move away from relying on myself. Give me the ability to know that it is You that I rely on. Be with me, Father, as I walk through these days. Guide me to the wisdom and faith in knowing that You are You, and that is all I could ever need. Amen

Fear is uneasiness over the things that have not
come to pass. It is the fear of the things that do
not exist in the present. People rarely fear the
game itself as much as they fear the loss of the
game. People rarely fear their coach as much as
they fear the upcoming practice after the loss
of a game, but what we must remember is that
we have the God that has overcome any fear
that we may have . . . the God that is greater
than any of our fears.

"*Haven't I commanded you: be strong and courageous? Do not be afraid or discouraged, for the Lord your God is with you wherever you go.*"
    Joshua 1:9

————

When I am afraid,
I will trust in you.
    Psalm 56:3

————

You did not receive a spirit of slavery to fall back into fear. Instead, you received the Spirit of adoption, by whom we cry out, "Abba, Father!"
    Romans 8:15

For God has not given us a spirit of fear, but one of power, love, and sound judgment.

   2 Timothy 1:7

———

Humble yourselves, therefore, under the mighty hand of God, so that he may exalt you at the proper time, casting all your cares on him, because he cares about you.

   1 Peter 5:6–7

Heavenly Father, I am afraid. There are things in my future that if I fail, I fear it will all be over. God, I know that there is no fear if I rest in You. Father, give me that comfort in knowing that I can rest in You, and that whatever may happen, will happen for a reason. Give me peace, Lord, so that I may know that with You, there is nothing I have to fear. Amen

Forgiveness means erasing the record of the wrong someone has done to you. Most would think that sports should be a place where things are easily forgivable, but ask any former athlete and they can relive the worst moment caused by another teammate: the missed pass, the bad kick, the weak block. Though these seem like tiny mistakes, they may have had major consequences. Scholarships and careers are often on the line for some of these athletes. Look to Scripture to know that forgiveness of others is not only important but necessary for recovery . . . whether that be on the field or off.

"Therefore I tell you, her many sins have been forgiven; that's why she loved much. But the one who is forgiven little, loves little."

Luke 7:47

———

Live in harmony with one another. Do not be proud; instead, associate with the humble. Do not be wise in your own estimation. Do not repay anyone evil for evil. Give careful thought to do what is honorable in everyone's eyes. If possible, as far as it depends on you, live at peace with everyone.

Romans 12:16–18

*Be kind and compassionate to one another,
forgiving one another, just as God also forgave you
in Christ.*

    Ephesians 4:32

---

*As God's chosen ones, holy and dearly loved, put on
compassion, kindness, humility, gentleness, and
patience, bearing with one another and forgiving
one another if anyone has a grievance against
another. Just as the Lord has forgiven you, so you
are also to forgive.*

    Colossians 3:12–13

Lord, I struggle with forgiving others. I feel that there are those around me that have wronged me and don't even care. Father, allow me to move past these feelings and move forward with You. Instill in me a heart that forgives those that have done wrong to me. Father, I know I have also harmed others with my actions. Allow them to forgive me. Father, drive me to work for reconciliation so that I may better serve You. Amen

How good it is to have a friend, a comrade, a welcomed rival. Most athletes will tell you that they can remember that person that helped to drive them to become better. Some will be honest enough to tell you that it was that sharpening from other players that made them the athlete they came to be. Friendship is one of the most amazing aspects of sports. They cheer when you succeed. They hurt when you fail, and they can even instill in you a passion to become better than you were yesterday. Scripture shows the importance of friendship. Pray. Thank God for the friends in your life, and pray even more that He will help you to be a friend to others.

Iron sharpens iron,
and one person sharpens another.
    Proverbs 27:17

———

Two are better than one because they have a good
reward for their efforts. For if either falls, his
companion can lift him up; but pity the one who
falls without another to lift him up.
    Ecclesiastes 4:9–10

———

Dear friends, let us love one another, because love is
from God, and everyone who loves has been born of
God and knows God.
    1 John 4:7

"No one has greater love than this: to lay down his life for his friends. You are my friends if you do what I command you. I do not call you servants anymore, because a servant doesn't know what his master is doing. I have called you friends, because I have made known to you everything I have heard from my Father."

John 15:13–15

———

Therefore encourage one another and build each other up as you are already doing.

1 Thessalonians 5:11

Father, thank You for friends. Thank You for putting those in my life that sharpen and strengthen me. Thank You for those special people that sharpen me, strengthen me, care for me, and love me. Lord, allow me to be a better friend to those around me. Instill in me a spirit that cares for those that You have put in my life. Amen

Great coaches and seasoned athletes understand grace better than most. Giving grace to those you lead is one of the most important things you can do for the success of your team. One of the greatest things that you can do for those less experienced than you is to give grace. Remember, God gives grace to us in the moments that we fail. Should we not use this knowledge in giving grace to others?

The law came along to multiply the trespass. But where sin multiplied, grace multiplied even more.
　　Romans 5:20

———

For sin will not rule over you, because you are not under the law but under grace.
　　Romans 6:14

———

Now if by grace, then it is not by works; otherwise grace ceases to be grace.
　　Romans 11:6

But he said to me, "My grace is sufficient for you, for my power is perfected in weakness." Therefore, I will most gladly boast all the more about my weaknesses, so that Christ's power may reside in me.

    2 Corinthians 12:9

———

For you are saved by grace through faith, and this is not from yourselves; it is God's gift—not from works, so that no one can boast.

    Ephesians 2:8–9

Father, I know that I need grace. I know that I am so far from perfect. Father, thank You for giving me grace when I fail. Father, instill in me a spirit that allows me to give grace to others when they let me down. Lord, give others the ability to give me grace whenever I fail them. Amen

Athletes can often see the consequence of impulsiveness. It is a weakness that shows up at least once in every game. Someone moves before the ball is snapped. Someone jumps too early. They move right when they should have moved left. In fact, it is a common strategy to take advantage of your opponent's impulsiveness. It is a weakness in competition, but it is even more so a weakness in life. God calls us to be patient, to be wise. You cannot be these things and, at the same time, have an impulsive spirit.

Discretion will watch over you,
and understanding will guard you.
It will rescue you from the way of evil—
from anyone who says perverse things,
    Proverbs 2:11–12

———

So if you have been raised with Christ, seek the
things above, where Christ is, seated at the right
hand of God. Set your minds on things above, not
on earthly things.
    Colossians 3:1–2

For we all stumble in many ways. If anyone does not stumble in what he says, he is mature, able also to control the whole body.

    James 3:2

———

Watch yourselves so you don't lose what we have worked for, but that you may receive a full reward. Anyone who does not remain in Christ's teaching but goes beyond it does not have God. The one who remains in that teaching, this one has both the Father and the Son.

    2 John 8–9

Lord Jesus, I have an impulsive spirit. Take that away from me, Lord. Replace it with a spirit of wisdom and patience so that I may have better discernment. Lord, teach me to put to rest the impulsive ways that cause me to make so many mistakes. Give me the wisdom to act with a more thoughtful attitude. Amen

Integrity can sometimes mean pointing out what you've done wrong that no one saw. Most of us have seen that integrity in a game. There was once a baseball player that walked up to a pair of arguing umpires on whether he had been safe or out. Though he didn't want to, he still walked up to the two of them and said that his foot had never touched the base when he had been tagged. Integrity comes with a heavy price, sometimes, but those that walk in integrity will never have to carry the weight of guilt.

The one who lives with integrity lives securely,
but whoever perverts his ways will be found out.
    Proverbs 10:9

———

Better the poor person who lives with integrity
than the rich one who distorts right and wrong.
    Proverbs 28:6

———

Indeed, we are giving careful thought to do what
is right, not only before the Lord but also before
people.
    2 Corinthians 8:21

Whatever you do, do it from the heart, as something done for the Lord and not for people, knowing that you will receive the reward of an inheritance from the Lord. You serve the Lord Christ.

   Colossians 3:23–24

———

Yet do this with gentleness and respect, keeping a clear conscience, so that when you are accused, those who disparage your good conduct in Christ will be put to shame.

   1 Peter 3:16

Heavenly Father, there are times that I don't always feel like doing the right thing. I struggle to do what is honorable when no one is looking. Father, put in me a spirit that drives me to walk with integrity. Allow me to do what is right even in the difficult moments when no one would know I had done wrong. Father, give me a spirit that strives for righteousness so that I may live a life that is more representative of You. Amen

Laziness is a quality that no one finds useful. In sports, it can often mean the difference between a win and a loss. Someone will occasionally win a game if they happen to be more talented, but no one is ever surprised when they see someone get beaten by the harder worker. Determination is normally the mark of the winner, and determination is never a quality found with a lazy person. God is no different on the matter; Scripture points to the need for hard work.

The slacker craves, yet has nothing,
but the diligent is fully satisfied.
> *Proverbs 13:4*

———

Whatever you do, do it from the heart, as something
done for the Lord and not for people, knowing that
you will receive the reward of an inheritance from
the Lord. You serve the Lord Christ.
> *Colossians 3:23–24*

The one who is lazy in his work
is brother to a vandal.
Proverbs 18:9

———

In fact, when we were with you, this is what we
commanded you: "If anyone isn't willing to work,
he should not eat."
2 Thessalonians 3:10

Lord, I am at a moment where I just want to do nothing. I know there are things I have to do, but God, I just want to take a nap, or watch TV or do anything that is not whatever needs to be done. Father, instill in me a spirit that will drive me to do what needs to be done. Drive me to fight complacency. Amen

No one likes a liar, and no one ever wants one as a teammate. If a player has used deception with his or her team, they can almost guarantee themselves that they will not have a successful season. It does not matter the level of your talent. If a team cannot trust you, they will not work hard for your success, even if it means that they may sacrifice their success. Trustworthiness is one of the most important things that a person can have. When people see it, they instinctively value you. The same goes for God, there is no place in His house for a liar.

No one who acts deceitfully
will live in my palace;
the one who tells lies
will not be retained here to guide me.
  Psalm 101:7

―――――

Lying lips are detestable to the LORD,
but faithful people are his delight.
  Proverbs 12:22

―――――

A false witness will not go unpunished,
and one who utters lies perishes.
  Proverbs 19:9

"For nothing is concealed that won't be revealed, and nothing hidden that won't be made known and brought to light."

    Luke 8:17

———

Do not lie to one another, since you have put off the old self with its practices and have put on the new self. You are being renewed in knowledge according to the image of your Creator.

    Colossians 3:9–10

Father, forgive me. I have lied to those around me. I have turned away from the truth and relied on lying to others. Father, I realize that my actions are causing me to lose the trust and confidence of others. Lord, allow me to come clean to those relationships I have dirtied with my lies. Give me the opportunities to make right what my lies have made wrong. Amen

MERCY

There is nothing quite like mercy. Most of us have seen it in one form or another, but there's something special about it from the perspective of sports. Most coaches normally punish their players for a loss. There was a coach that would make his players run laps for every point they lost by, but I'll never forget what this same coach said the day after the team lost a major play-off game. He looked at his team and said, "You lost the game, but you gave everything to it. . . . I won't ask for more." Mercy was given to that team . . . not because they necessarily deserved it. They lost! The coach, however, showed them mercy in spite of their failings. God is the same. He shows us mercy and love in spite of ourselves.

"Blessed are the merciful, for they will be shown mercy."

   Matthew 5:7

———

"Go and learn what this means: I desire mercy and not sacrifice. For I didn't come to call the righteous, but sinners."

   Matthew 9:13

———

Therefore, let us approach the throne of grace with boldness, so that we may receive mercy and find grace to help us in time of need.

   Hebrews 4:16

Speak and act as those who are to be judged by the law of freedom. For judgment is without mercy to the one who has not shown mercy. Mercy triumphs over judgment.

  James 2:12–13

———

Blessed be the God and Father of our Lord Jesus Christ. Because of his great mercy he has given us new birth into a living hope through the resurrection of Jesus Christ from the dead.

  1 Peter 1:3

Lord, thank You for having mercy on me. I know I don't deserve it. Father, I know that there are those in my life that I need to show mercy as You have shown me. Lord, soften my heart so that I may show mercy to those that have failed me. Allow me to look at those that have not been perfect and see myself. Have me be reminded that I am not perfect, and it is because of that, that I need to show mercy because mercy was shown to me. Amen

The motives of a coach can mean everything in regard to the team, and those motives are obvious. If the only motivation is winning, winning will be their greatest celebration and losing, their greatest devastation. Some teams care about fun. You'll see laughter and smiles, but not a lot of respect for wins and losses. Some teams, however, care about creating good people. Those teams chase after the quality of the player. Wins come with celebration; losses with remorse, but the focus is on teaching the player sportsmanship, respect, and hard work. Our motives say a lot about our walk, but they are always obvious.

But the LORD said to Samuel, "Do not look at his appearance or his stature because I have rejected him. Humans do not see what the LORD sees, for humans see what is visible, but the LORD sees the heart."

1 Samuel 16:7

———

All a person's ways seem right to him, but the LORD weighs hearts.

Proverbs 21:2

———

For am I now trying to persuade people, or God? Or am I striving to please people? If I were still trying to please people, I would not be a servant of Christ.

Galatians 1:10

Do nothing out of selfish ambition or conceit, but in humility consider others as more important than yourselves.

Philippians 2:3

———

Instead, just as we have been approved by God to be entrusted with the gospel, so we speak, not to please people, but rather God, who examines our hearts.

1 Thessalonians 2:4

Lord God, make my motivations pure. Father, I know that I have put my priorities in the wrong places. Father, remind me daily to know that everything I do should be to honor You. Lord, fix my heart and my desires so that I may better serve You. Direct my mind to focus on the things that You would have me focus on. Father, make my motivations the ones that You would have for me. Amen

Obedience does not mean that you're a slave by any means, but there is an importance to doing what you're coached to do. Obedience comes from trust. You may not understand why you run this route, or why you run left instead of right, but you do as you're coached. This obedience is a product of trust and faith that your coach knows best. In your life, do you live obediently to God, or do you not trust that God knows best?

I have chosen the way of truth;
I have set your ordinances before me.
   Psalm 119:30

———

"If you love me, you will keep my commands."
   John 14:15

———

Peter and the apostles replied, "We must obey God
rather than people."
   Acts 5:29

The one who keeps his commands remains in him, and he in him. And the way we know that he remains in us is from the Spirit he has given us.

    1 John 3:24

———

For this is what love for God is: to keep his commands. And his commands are not a burden, because everyone who has been born of God conquers the world. This is the victory that has conquered the world: our faith.

    1 John 5:3–4

Father, I know that You are right. I know that what You say is true. Lord, teach me to live in obedience to you. Put in me a desire to live according to Your Word. Father, I know that You see a picture that I have only a glimpse of. Allow me to live a life that recognizes that. Guide me, Lord, so that I may be more obedient . . . not out of fear, but out of love. Amen

PATIENCE

Most high schools have been put in a rough situation from time to time as far as performance is concerned. Most of us have seen how a school will have an all-star team because of their seniors, but when those seniors graduate, there is this dry period where the school deals with the next season being filled with losses. Those without patience will see this as a time of loss and nothing more, but the wise will see this as a time of rebuilding, a time of preparation, a time to readjust and move forward. You yourself may be in a time of frustration; is this a time of loss in which you're doomed to reside? Or is it a time to be patient and rebuild?

The end of a matter is better than its beginning;
a patient spirit is better than a proud spirit.

    Ecclesiastes 7:8

———

Now if we hope for what we do not see, we eagerly
wait for it with patience.

    Romans 8:25

———

My dear brothers and sisters, understand this:
Everyone should be quick to listen, slow to speak,
and slow to anger, for human anger does not
accomplish God's righteousness.

    James 1:19–20

Therefore, brothers and sisters, be patient until the Lord's coming. See how the farmer waits for the precious fruit of the earth and is patient with it until it receives the early and the late rains. You also must be patient. Strengthen your hearts, because the Lord's coming is near.

    James 5:7–8

———

The Lord does not delay his promise, as some understand delay, but is patient with you, not wanting any to perish but all to come to repentance.

    2 Peter 3:9

Lord, I hate waiting. I am so ready to be where I want to be, but I know that the reason I am in a time of waiting is because there is something You want me to learn. Father, allow me to move with patience. Allow me to wait, God. Bring in me a spirit that knows that there is a time for everything, and that this is a time that You would have for me to be patient. Amen

If you were to ask a coach to choose between the player that can throw a football sixty yards but only comes to two practices a week or the player that can only throw thirty-five yards but will stay thirty minutes after every practice to get better, which player do you think the coach will choose? Never giving up is one of the most important aspects that a person can have, let alone an athlete. The same goes for us. God calls us to be the type of people that never give up, that never settle, that always make every step a step that is moving forward.

And not only that, but we also rejoice in our
afflictions, because we know that affliction
produces endurance, endurance produces proven
character, and proven character produces hope. This
hope will not disappoint us, because God's love
has been poured out in our hearts through the Holy
Spirit who was given to us.

    Romans 5:3–5

———

Consider it a great joy, my brothers and sisters,
whenever you experience various trials, because
you know that the testing of your faith produces
endurance. And let endurance have its full effect,
so that you may be mature and complete, lacking
nothing.

    James 1:2–4

Let us not get tired of doing good, for we will reap at the proper time if we don't give up.

  Galatians 6:9

———

Therefore, since we also have such a large cloud of witnesses surrounding us, let us lay aside every hindrance and the sin that so easily ensnares us. Let us run with endurance the race that lies before us, keeping our eyes on Jesus, the source and perfecter of our faith. For the joy that lay before him, he endured the cross, despising the shame, and sat down at the right hand of the throne of God.

  Hebrews 12:1–2

Father, I am weary. I am so ready for this time to be over. My mind, body, and spirit are all tired. Father, allow me to push through this tiredness. Have me discover new found energy that will allow me to stand up and keep moving forward. Father, give me the drive to know that there is a finish line on the other side of this valley. Thank You, Father, for being with me as I push forward. Amen

We spend a lot of time preparing for a game. We exercise; we study the other team; and we plan out the future moments in upcoming games. A dedicated athlete will give hours of time to a sport, and yet, will struggle with finding peace. Where does one find this peace? We find it through constant communication with God. We pray to God to ease the tension in our hearts. We pray for wisdom and confidence. You can do everything in your own power to make sure that everything is going to go according to plan, but nothing can ease the soul quite like prayer.

"Whenever you pray, you must not be like the hypocrites, because they love to pray standing in the synagogues and on the street corners to be seen by people. . . . But when you pray, go into your private room, shut your door, and pray to your Father who is in secret. And your Father who sees in secret will reward you. When you pray, don't babble like the Gentiles, since they imagine they'll be heard for their many words. . . .

"Therefore, you should pray like this: Our Father in heaven, your name be honored as holy. Your kingdom come. Your will be done on earth as it is in heaven. Give us today our daily bread. And forgive us our debts, as we also have forgiven our debtors. And do not bring us into temptation, but deliver us from the evil one.

"For if you forgive others their offenses, your heavenly Father will forgive you as well. But if you don't forgive others, your Father will not forgive your offenses."

Matthew 6:5–15

*If you remain in me and my words remain in you,
ask whatever you want and it will be done for you.*
    John 15:7

———

*In the same way the Spirit also helps us in our
weakness, because we do not know what to pray for
as we should, but the Spirit himself intercedes for
us with unspoken groanings.*
    Romans 8:26

———

*Don't worry about anything, but in everything,
through prayer and petition with thanksgiving,
present your requests to God.*
    Philippians 4:6

Lord Jesus, I come to You at this time to discover more about You. Father, there are things in my life that I worry about. There are times that I know I cannot do things on my own. Lord, I know that there are times that I need something more than what this world can ever give me. Lord, thank You for being there. Thank You for listening. In times of fear, frustration, worry, and weariness, thank You for allowing me to come before You and pray. Amen

Sports are one of the few instances where you will see people paint their faces and scream with all they have for the sake of their pride in their team. There's a bit of fun in team pride; most understand that. The problem with pride, however, comes when a person begins to believe that they are legitimately better than others. Pride, after all, is simply the act of putting oneself over others. Being proud of your team is fine, but truly believing that a person is better than others is detrimental to one's character.

When arrogance comes, disgrace follows,
but with humility comes wisdom.
　　Proverbs 11:2

———

Everyone with a proud heart is detestable to the Lord;
be assured, he will not go unpunished.
　　Proverbs 16:5

———

A person's pride will humble him,
but a humble spirit will gain honor.
　　Proverbs 29:23

Live in harmony with one another. Do not be proud; instead, associate with the humble. Do not be wise in your own estimation.

    Romans 12:16

———

For if anyone considers himself to be something when he is nothing, he deceives himself.

    Galatians 6:3

Lord, I have become someone that believes I am better than others. Father, I know that I cannot live this way. I know that You would not have me live this way. Lord God, take this prideful spirit away from me and replace it with humility. Put in me, the daily knowledge that I am someone that is not above anyone else. Amen

Most team sports have some level of protection as a major part of the game. Football, basketball, and soccer all hold the same concept of looking out for the player with the ball. They often involve a clearing of a path for the ball and the player in control of it. If there is no protection, a player can find himself outnumbered on a level in which he cannot defend, but if a team performs the way it should, the player should not have to worry about a situation they cannot handle on their own. God is the same way with temptation, He will never put you against something that you cannot defeat.

Protect me as the pupil of your eye;
hide me in the shadow of your wings.
    Psalm 17:8

———

The angel of the LORD encamps
around those who fear him, and rescues them.
    Psalm 34:7

———

The mountains surround Jerusalem
and the LORD surrounds his people,
both now and forever.
    Psalm 125:2

The name of the LORD is a strong tower;
the righteous run to it and are protected.
    Proverbs 18:10

———

But the Lord is faithful; he will strengthen and
guard you from the evil one.
    2 Thessalonians 3:3

Heavenly Father, thank You for Your protection. There are so many times when the bad could have happened, or the bad could have become worse, and yet, You protected me. Lord, I know that there are many moments ahead that You already know will put me in hard situations, but I already have faith that You will be with me. Thank You for Your protection, Lord. I pray it may always continue. Amen

If you talk to any wrestler, they will tell you self-control is a necessity. They go through weeks and weeks of dieting just for the success of one day. They can also reference a time they didn't show self-control and how they would do anything to have that moment back. One pound too light or too heavy can mean the difference between being the heaviest person on the mat or the lightest. Most of us understand that self-control is so important for our physical health, but it does so much for our spirit as well. Pray that God instills in you a spirit of self-control.

*A person who does not control his temper
is like a city whose wall is broken down.*

    Proverbs 25:28

———

*No temptation has come upon you except what is
common to humanity. But God is faithful; he will
not allow you to be tempted beyond what you are
able, but with the temptation he will also provide a
way out so that you may be able to bear it.*

    1 Corinthians 10:13

*Finally brothers and sisters, whatever is
true, whatever is honorable, whatever is just,
whatever is pure, whatever is lovely, whatever is
commendable—if there is any moral excellence and
if there is anything praiseworthy—dwell on these
things.*
    Philippians 4:8

———

*Be sober-minded, be alert. Your adversary the devil
is prowling around like a roaring lion, looking for
anyone he can devour.*
    1 Peter 5:8

Father, I struggle with controlling my actions. I have lived selfishly. Father, forgive me for my lack of self-control. Forgive me for acting with a heart that only cares about itself. Lord, instill in me a wisdom that allows me to see the importance of self-control. Allow me to say no to the things that I shouldn't desire, and drive me to say yes to the things You would have for me. Amen

When we think about strength, we normally go straight to physical prowess. In some sports, your entire worth is dependent upon the amount of weight your body can move. Physical strength is important, but we rarely take the time to focus on spiritual strength. In fact, when we do, we sometimes mistake it for "mental toughness." The mark of a strong person, athletic or not, is their ability to take on the difficult situations in life and continue to press on. This is something that comes from one's spirit, that is a strength that only God can provide.

My flesh and my heart may fail,
but God is the strength of my heart,
my portion forever.
    Psalm 73:26

———

But he said to me, "My grace is sufficient for you,
for my power is perfected in weakness." Therefore,
I will most gladly boast all the more about my
weaknesses, so that Christ's power may reside
in me. So I take pleasure in weaknesses, insults,
hardships, persecutions, and in difficulties, for
the sake of Christ. For when I am weak, then I am
strong.
    2 Corinthians 12:9–10

If I say, "My foot is slipping,"
your faithful love will support me, LORD.
    Psalm 94:18

———

Consider it a great joy, my brothers and sisters,
whenever you experience various trials, because
you know that the testing of your faith produces
endurance.
    James 1:2–3

Lord Jesus, there are obstacles in my life that seem insurmountable. I feel like there is no way that I can overcome the things that are before me, and God, I know I'm right. I know that I cannot defeat the odds with my strength alone. I know that it is only through You that I can beat what lies before me. Lord, give me strength as I take on these hardships. Amen

The biggest struggle with success is the forgetting of who gets the credit. There are so many times that we will look to our own abilities when thinking about our success. We think that it was because of our training and our preparation that guaranteed success, but the fact is that all of those training sessions, all of those moments of preparation, were only available because God gave you the drive and gifts to be able to create that success. Remember that when you succeed, it is God that allowed for those moments.

Take delight in the LORD,
and he will give you your heart's desires.
    Psalm 37:4

———

Commit your activities to the LORD,
and your plans will be established.
    Proverbs 16:3

"For what will it benefit someone if he gains the whole world yet loses his life? Or what will anyone give in exchange for his life? For the Son of Man is going to come with his angels in the glory of his Father, and then he will reward each according to what he has done."

    Matthew 16:26–27

———

Humble yourselves before the Lord, and he will exalt you.

    James 4:10

Father, thank You for the success in my life. Thank You for giving me the moments that have allowed me to grow to where I am today. Lord, allow me to remember that each moment of success is a moment that You've allowed to happen. Father, continue to give me these moments of growth and remind me that whatever success may come is because of You. Amen

Any team will tell you that one of the most important things you need for success is trust. If you cannot trust a teammate, there is almost no chance for victory. When someone passes the ball, they trust the ball will be caught. When someone runs a route, they trust that someone will be there to block for them. There is an obvious level of trust that comes with that team bond. You do your job, and trust that someone else will do theirs. We so naturally trust our teammates, but also remember how good it is to put your trust in God, that trust is one that never fails.

The person who trusts in the LORD, whose confidence indeed is the LORD, is blessed. He will be like a tree planted by water: it sends its roots out toward a stream, it doesn't fear when heat comes, and its foliage remains green. It will not worry in a year of drought or cease producing fruit.

Jeremiah 17:7–8

———

Wait for the LORD;
be strong, and let your heart be courageous.
Wait for the LORD.

Psalm 27:14

I will be with you when you pass through the waters, and when you pass through the rivers, they will not overwhelm you. You will not be scorched when you walk through the fire, and the flame will not burn you.

    Isaiah 43:2

———

And my God will supply all your needs according to his riches in glory in Christ Jesus.

    Philippians 4:19

———

This is the confidence we have before him: If we ask anything according to his will, he hears us.

    1 John 5:14

Lord, I struggle. I put up walls to protect me from others. These walls have kept me from loving. Father, break down these walls around me. Allow me to love and trust others. Give me the strength to move past the fears of being let down, and Father, give me the strength to trust You. I know that You are good. I know that You are with me. Thank You, Father. Thank You for always being there. Thank You for being the one I put my trust in. Amen

Victory and loss are imperative to the sport experience. It's so important for us to understand that sometimes we will lose. We may not always win, but something that we are guaranteed is victory in Christ. Competitions and contests will come and go. You may win, and you may lose; but the ultimate battle, the ultimate competition, has been fought and won by Jesus Christ. Though there may be days that seem hard, take joy in knowing that the game is settled. The battle is won.

*For the LORD your God is the one who goes with you
to fight for you against your enemies to give you
victory.*

Deuteronomy 20:4

———

*Though a righteous person falls seven times,
he will get up,
but the wicked will stumble into ruin.*

Proverbs 24:16

———

*"I have told you these things so that in me you may
have peace. You will have suffering in this world.
Be courageous! I have conquered the world."*

John 16:33

*The sting of death is sin, and the power of sin is the
law. But thanks be to God, who gives us the victory
through our Lord Jesus Christ!*
  1 Corinthians 15:56–57

———

*Then I heard a loud voice from the throne: Look,
God's dwelling is with humanity, and he will
live with them. They will be his peoples, and God
himself will be with them and will be their God.
He will wipe away every tear from their eyes. Death
will be no more; grief, crying, and pain will be no
more, because the previous things have passed
away.*
  Revelation 21:3–4

Father, thank You. You have given me triumph. You have given me victory. Lord, thank You for blessing me with success. Father, I know that in this life there are highs and lows . . . wins and losses; but God, it is in You that we find true victory. Father, no matter what may come, give me the peace of mind in knowing that it is through You that we have the final victory . . . that even in the times when I feel like the world is winning . . . it is You that has already won. Amen

Some players rely on their talents; some rely on their brains. Coaches definitely appreciate talent, but more often than not, they will want the player that can think their way through plays. They will want the one that can make decisions wisely. Wisdom is one of the most sought after qualities a player can have. The reason? Talent fades, but wisdom has the potential to constantly grow. Consult Scripture to grow in that wisdom.

Teach us to number our days carefully
so that we may develop wisdom in our hearts.
   Psalm 90:12

———

Do not be conformed to this age, but be transformed
by the renewing of your mind, so that you may
discern what is the good, pleasing, and perfect will
of God.
   Romans 12:2

Yet to those who are called, both Jews and Greeks,
Christ is the power of God and the wisdom of God,
because God's foolishness is wiser than human
wisdom, and God's weakness is stronger than
human strength.
   1 Corinthians 1:24–25

———

Now if any of you lacks wisdom, he should
ask God—who gives to all generously and
ungrudgingly—and it will be given to him.
   James 1:5

Heavenly Father, I have made poor decisions. I have thought irrationally. I have acted without wisdom. Lord, give me the foresight in knowing what to do in these difficult situations. Allow me to have discernment in the moments that require judgment. Father, work through me. Give me the wisdom to act in a way that is good and right in Your eyes. Amen

Many athletes can remember a time when they worried. Whether a rival team is coming up on the schedule, or a playoff game is going to mean the continuation or end of a season, or even something as simple as making the team in the first place. Sports can create some precarious situations. Something that we have to come to terms with, however, is that the outcome is going to be whatever it will be, but the one constant that will always be is God. He always has been and always will be. In that, we can find peace.

"Therefore I tell you: Don't worry about your life, what you will eat or what you will drink; or about your body, what you will wear. Isn't life more than food and the body more than clothing? Consider the birds of the sky: They don't sow or reap or gather into barns, yet your heavenly Father feeds them. Aren't you worth more than they? Can any of you add one moment to his life-span by worrying?"

Matthew 6:25–27

———

The Lord answered her, "Martha, Martha, you are worried and upset about many things, but one thing is necessary. Mary has made the right choice, and it will not be taken away from her."

Luke 10:41–42

We know that all things work together for the good of those who love God, who are called according to his purpose.

Romans 8:28

———

Don't worry about anything, but in everything, through prayer and petition with thanksgiving, present your requests to God. And the peace of God, which surpasses all understanding, will guard your hearts and minds in Christ Jesus.

Philippians 4:6–7

Father, I am worried. I have allowed fear to creep into my life, and now I feel that I have been put in a place where I can't move forward. I worry about the future, Lord. I worry that I will not be able to handle what lies before me. Father, put in me an understanding, a peace, that knows that whatever may come, You are with me. Amen